Foreclosure

Gregory Lawless

Back Pages Publishers
289 Moody Street
Waltham, Massachusetts.

Text Design: Michael Shapiro

Library of Congress Cataloging-in-Publication Data
ISBN 978-0-615-77792-4

www.backpagesbooks.com

1 2 3 4 5 6 7 8 9 10

Contents

Factoryville Eclogue

November fields. Ice-withered parsley and wild
alfalfa after a morning of freezing rain. I look
for heart-leaved asters in the open woods,
with rust-dusted scissors and a plastic bag. They go
in an old glass inkwell on my wife's nightstand
and last eight days in water. *Winter flowers,*
she says, but that's not quite right. I don't
correct her. Winter is her business. Fall
is mine. Christmas ferns wither well
before December. I keep a bed of them
in a bucket out back and watch ravens
snatch the leaflets for their nests. Parabolic birds.
The color of stories. Maybe not. Everyone has a neighbor
who shoots them. Not everyone has a neighbor,
thank God. Thank God for what? For winter, the sound
of ravens sorting ferns in the snow. My wife thinks
I look too much. At what? *You look too much,*
that's all. It's fall. A truck from Dalton Lumber's
tipped over in the field. Everyone is alive.
They left an hour ago and left their lumber. Stacks
of blond planks stained with ice, fifty yards
from dead asters. What do I tell her? They were out
of flowers. *Who are they*? she'll say. The field, fall,
who knows? They were out. I take some dead ones
back, my scissors frozen shut. *Thanks.* Thank
God for what? The field-kill dressed in ice, a lumber
spill, generations of ravens in the firs. No snow
yet. Is that a blessing? I don't know. Who's in charge
of these blessings?

Factoryville Anabasis

Three great blue heron eggs chewed apart by young raccoons between sleeves of jewelweed and slender nettle.

I used to paint vulture eggs in Petaluma.

They laid them in the loft of an abandoned barn nearby and sometimes in the crotch of a fallen pepper tree.

I never got the brown spots quite right, like flecks of blood on a washed-out white cotton shirt.

I used to hang our wash on the bare branches of an old arroyo willow.

My wife said her shirts smelled like leaves, but I could never tell.

The coyotes here in Pennsylvania will eat raccoons during long, lean winters.

I never know what I'm hearing in the woods.

The shells of heron eggs like broken lakes.

I can see the creek where the raccoons clean their feet.

Low water now, dry summer: lures, beer bottles, and a pair of broken oars on the banks.

The grocery store in town sells gopher poison and heavy-duty grease for tractor gears.

I haven't seen a vulture egg in years.

Riprap

I was thinking of Tolstoy's Austerlitz—
how the soldiers at first were merely tired
of marching in their shredded boots
before the bombs whistled into earthworks;
the hussars needling their horses between
missiles; some troops laughing as they loaded
mortars and tamped their musket shot
down errant barrels. Then, the sudden
amputees begging to be flung upon a cart
and stacked in hospitals. How someone forgets
to burn a bridge and the empire flickers eastward
after that. I'd love to see some cities before
they're cinders merely. In Srebrenica
the water towers scored black as winter
oaks. In college, I wanted to go to Baghdad.
My friend's dad was in the embassy
in Istanbul and said he went "There" once
on business before "all this messiness."
His prudish diction and clean fingernails. "I loved
the markets There," he said, careful not
to remember much. Poor loud-mouthed
spook, selling fake explosives in some shattered
souk. He probably believed they believed
he was Russian. I was thinking of Tolstoy's
princes, and how the most beautiful passages
are less about peace than dailyness:
a wolf hunt, say, or waiting for horses
in some forgotten inn, a duel between
two idle rivals. I was thinking about this
when I was laying riprap at my father's house,
packing stone into the soft banks
of my father's ditches. The gnat-busy
misery of summer labor, the work
I hated with childish force. How in a moment
of swelter I blamed him for the sad fact

of work itself, the drone and sacrifice,
and went home hot and silent. He called me
later and said he'd finally killed the deer
that ate his marigolds. Next spring, he said,
they'd bloom much better. He's getting better
at promising things. His history sinks down to me
after after-dinner cups of tea: a paper route
from fifty years ago, or the cost of cigarettes in Idaho,
in 1971, when he spent the summer sawing
lumber and daydreaming about the draft. Poor
bland Canada, he thought, thinking of his future.
When Nixon ditched the draft, my father
was free. Poor kings, thought Tolstoy,
the slaves of history. When my father
flicked his cigarette at the dry weeds
like a curse, I thought of Moscow's fires,
the trampled winter wheat, and all
the wrecked estates in the vast October
pages of *War and Peace*. He seemed happy
then, my father. He said he liked his new wife
better than the last. But he is agony
to read. What would you think, he asked
me once, if Nixon saved your life?

Notebooks

Light built of ghost bricks. Clatter of magpie and Canada jay. A horse steps into a lake, stops, bows low for water. Knuckles of stars, dry parings of ago. Singed birds, like crust withering, bread just smoke you can eat. Pine trees comprised of idle daggers. These hours, barn-dark and God-hot, no good for going away. Water, wind, the breath between your teeth. Your tongue's back broken. Your blood tied in a knot. Sing, that is, until they tell you to stop.

Notebooks

Gold looming. A terrain not giving up to sea or being seen.

~

I toss this swatch of birds with a whistle.

~

Far-feeling, like watching a penny fall from a building.

~

And the wind / keep it / from killing.

Foreclosure

Jar full of screws and washers. Moisture clouding the glass with remembered breath. Rusted-swing-set color of sunset. The swing set is blue. Hammers, nails, tires. Country car in the crabgrass by the shed. Crows in the tulip trees. Flood waters parting the grey planks of the wood bridge nearby. Apple empires and toppled walls. Hammock screws twisted into pines. Pitch pouring into threading and grooves.

~

You call me back to the car. The way a man loses his hands between ladder rungs. You with your guardrail beauty. Sloping gently out of view. With your dents and etchings. I watch the dust fluster the driveway. The snakes of weather stripping lash the soft tires. We back up a long way to the road.

Straw Lady

She stutters from the brush. A tire iron under wing. A lug-nut love. A dress for running away. A bramble-and-briar way of running away. With a sleeve of grease. With the sere arousals of cattails. She with the yard couch and possum scat on dented leather. A pan for gathering rain. A poultice of field weeds. Brushings of mustard and dandelion seed in her slack hair. She sleeps in the yard car and steams the glass with bent dreams. Mice chew the wires away. They foul the console and she feeds them wild hazelnuts and blackberries crushed to seed. They bite her and she doesn't bleed.

Heart's Leak

Sleet pelts the cucumber patch. I patch the heart's leak with thatch and wet hickory leaves. Elm memories smear into firs. Away-going birds, we say. We foster seed. We fester into winter. Plastic sheeting rains down the panes.

Notebooks

I tweeze frags of tick parts from my ankles once they've drowned in gleams of Vaseline. *If I could die in a gleaming,* I sing, dropping the blood-black bodies in the sink.

Crow heart, silo high

Crow heart, silo high, mid careening. Thermals flicker finger feathers. A blink of tar. Plane pulse through cloudbank and what after that? A red vanishing. I am afraid to fly, to look down on my dreams: the seeming all bricked with blue. Lightning eye high. Crow weather trading shadows for severed breezes. For shares of uninhabitable sky.

Foreclosure

Gypsum dust and rifted sheetrock. Splayed joist, looks lightning struck. Copper pipes coil up to spout. Some ancient drip. Pink flamingoes stab the grass outside. Villages of ash trees savoring ravens. Lawn orbs all bb-shot and winter cracked. Wren haven in the mailbox, bird shit on the welcome mat. What can't live in what? I take the fake chrysanthemums for my wife. I take a cigar box full of shells and the fake brass plating from the mail slot. The door breathes in and out.

Knife, Fire, Map

Loon howl, some filings of moon still. What batters me awake? My wife takes a picture of daybreak. A lace shies into eyelets. The ankle creaks. A mistake. The facts of ligament and snap. We pack a back-pack in the dark. Knife, fire, map. Walking stick like a missing bone that God forgot. Blind strikes into ferns. Fear-trees, forty fathers high. The wind makes a ship sound, a hurt keel, a creaking past sleep. Our heel-strikes like hearts in the ground.

Tremor

As though reading the light and remembering the ending.

Definition

By ladder I mean to fall at one's leisure.

Reform

You commission someone to paint a picture of the worst thing you've ever done.

Notebooks

Beams, sawn wood, awakening grain. Curtains grieving across / expositions of frost.

~

A glass-built dream. Grass shoots, ice-crippled, hobbled with rime.

~

Birdlime beneath the eaves. Prewinter fear. Some teapot-shrill bird in the broken oak.

~

The kind of cold that—

~

Teapot unhanding its steam.

On the sill, sunlight bleaches dead beetles / the color of wheat.

Lure

Two lures in the trees / A pair of hooks there / and fishing line too fine to see

Foreclosure

Yard tires and washing tubs. Twin gas tanks painted like Angus bulls. Green things writhing in the meantime of the sun.

The shed is full of grudges. Lawnmowers and hanging blades. Oil-cans and rags.

Images dusking, going gray with rage.

I clean my glasses. Some grease is gone, but the scratches stay.

Definition

By book, I mean the space between fields. I mean the body like a bookmark keeping the page. I mean a chapter of sage and cloudberry and ash. I mean a chapter of winter, months later. I mean a climax of storms and the falling action of the snow. I mean it is dark, and you are running at breathless speeds. It is night, and you are trying to read.

Pipes

Gas company trucks sucking water from the river. Houses the shape of fires, slumping into weeds. I speak between disasters. I smear the landscape with a dream and ask it to remember. The gas trucks thunder our surrender. Daymare, rigs, and dynamite. Shale fracking apart. Landscape like a gas truck driving into dream. Sulfur water, hell fire in the streams. The gas goes down to Texas, where I have never been. Silver pipes bullet the landscape. They silver our surrender. The rigs light up at night like cruise ships in the trees. Dream collisions and revisions of water. Elisions of trees. They drill until they're out of me.

Foreclosure Prayer

Panes with crescent slices. Front door pocked with shot. The door-knob hot from sun, as though from fire within. I stop and knock a sick bat from the eaves with a wing of pipe. His flight, erratic, daft, like a card flicked into wind. So my own flight herein. Knock, knock. The wind. Rats. Scat on the torn corners of the couch. The teaspoon on the table holds a teaspoon of rain. I stare through roofrot at the sky, God's eye, and stuff a tunnel of newspaper inside to blind it dry.

Definition

When I say I want to save her, I mean from far away.

Trees and Fields

Two boys nail a white cotton sheet between two hickory trunks.

They draw a pair of human figures there with magic markers—no toes or fingers—then smack the marker people back with shot and slugs.

Their hearts are rags.

Twenty bite marks chew each gut and crotch.

They shoot until the faces fray and all you see are trees and fields through the flaps.

When the sheet falls, finally, they just shoot the trees and fields.

The Birds of Northeastern Pennsylvania

He called them *slaves of sky* and threw his seed across the graves.

He cursed them into trees.

He said their whole life was showing off, and it was. He said their flying made him tired.

At dawn, he held a sobbing rifle like a stack of flowers.

Thirty-three he counted in the tulip tree, then clapped two cans together to make them go away.

They flew away and came back again.

They came back and flew away.

Factoryville Eclogue

Morning, I ate five slices of browning apple, and then, hunger gone, walked into the field, mindful all the while of ticks and scrap.

I remembered the stories: boys gouging their feet on the teeth of a junked thresher, one dying days later.

The bites of nightmare spiders.

People gathered in the grass to fuck or smoke from glowing foil.

I went to find my uncle's starter pistol, snub-nosed, black, with a dull red snout.

He threw it there, one drunken twilight, after he pretended to shoot his second wife, for her insolence, in the face.

(This was 1993. I was fourteen. Nothing could be explained to me.)

(Maybe that is how my uncle felt about his wife, that only demonstration would suffice.)

Afterward, he walked into the woods, which he knew like a strange neighbor who does things, in silence, the same way, hour after hour.

Months later he came back, looking for his gun. He said, *I need it to scare the pigeons from my barn.*

You can blame anything on uncles. Footfalls in the brush. A crumpled aunt. A year you'd like to forget.

The grass was heavy. The waste stretched as far as I understood.

Acres of metal, freaked with dew, all looked the same in the wet sunlight. And I bent to seize each gleaming thing I could.

Acknowledgements

Many thanks to *The Journal, The Cincinnati Review, InDigest, Thrush, Salamander, Devil's Lake* and *South Dakota Review* for publishing select poems from this manuscript. Great thanks to my parents and Jen for their love and support.

Gregory Lawless is a graduate of the Iowa Writers' Workshop and the author of *I Thought I Was New Here*. His poems have appeared in *Third Coast, The National Poetry Review, Sonora Review, The Journal, The Cincinnati Review, Devil's Lake,* and many others. He lives in Waltham, Massachusetts.

CPSIA information can be obtained
at www.ICGtesting.com
Printed in the USA
LVIC04n1204200114
370093LV00002B/2
* 9 7 8 0 6 1 5 7 7 7 9 2 4 *